# Seasons from God

### Ron Jonson

**VANTAGE PRESS**
New York

FIRST EDITION

All rights reserved, including the right of
reproduction in whole or in part in any form.

Copyright © 2007 by Ron Jonson

Published by Vantage Press, Inc.
419 Park Ave. South, New York, NY 10016

Manufactured in the United States of America
ISBN: 0-533-15442-1

Library of Congress Catalog Card No.: 2006920341

0 9 8 7 6 5 4 3 2 1

To all who may enjoy

Dedicated
To the gal who pulled me thru

# Contents

*Preface* — vii
*Acknowledgment* — ix

| | |
|---|---|
| The Request | 1 |
| The Goal | 2 |
| Spirits | 3 |
| A Prophesy (I) | 5 |
| View from This Side | 6 |
| The Card (I) | 7 |
| A Prophesy (II) | 8 |
| Friendships | 9 |
| The Tree | 10 |
| Our Struggle | 12 |
| The Visit (I) | 13 |
| Letter to Pamela | 14 |
| A Prophesy (III) | 15 |
| The Coming | 16 |
| The Statement | 17 |
| Our Stay | 18 |
| A Christmas Letter | 19 |
| The Separation | 20 |
| Mary | 21 |
| My Psalm | 22 |
| In Passing | 23 |
| The Storm | 24 |
| Of Loving | 25 |
| The Card (II) | 26 |

| | |
|---|---|
| Two Towers | 27 |
| Letting Go | 28 |
| November | 29 |
| The Visit (II) | 30 |
| Fact or Friction | 32 |
| Preparations | 34 |
| The Vision | 35 |
| Jesus Was a Cowboy | 36 |
| The Glow | 38 |
| The Rapture | 39 |
| The Trade | 40 |
| Shields | 41 |
| The Parable | 42 |
| Weaver | 43 |
| Crucifixion | 44 |
| Of Christmas (I) | 46 |
| Your Gift | 47 |
| The Thank You | 48 |
| Of Christmas (II) | 49 |
| Christmas 2000 | 50 |
| Free Will | 51 |
| Vision of a Child | 52 |
| My Shelter from the Storm | 53 |

# Preface

This nation stands alone as one that drew a people from all lands and countries to struggle and form a union united under one God. In ignorance they made slaves of some and placed others on small plots of land they called reservations. In ignorance they took all the buffalo and all the White Pine and all the fish and game. So, laws were formed and followed and slavery ended and game were protected and reservations formed their own governments. And God smiled upon this country, but for a short time. For somewhere in its growing, this nation's leaders bent truths, relaxed laws and allowed "God" to be removed from all aspects of our society. And a breakdown of society occurred. And the majority sat quietly by as the minorities marched by with banners and took control. They now have our children and what is being taught to them will surely expand the breakdown. And the nation that will be created shall surely fall, for without the love of God it will decay away. Enclosed between these covers are thoughts that, if but one be swayed, shall be a triumph.

# Acknowledgment

Jesus, Son of God

## The Request

The Lord saith; "Follow!"
And I in turn asked, "Where?"
And the Lord replied, "Why is it thou hast asked?"
There was long silence . . .
"I wondered should I bring my bow and quiver?"
And the Lord asked, "Would'st it bring more comfort than I can offer?"
There was long silence . . .
"I will not bring my bow, let's go!"

# The Goal

Take Lord my earnings,
all that I'll gain;
I'll trade for a mountain
of clover and rain.

# Spirits

If life has dealt a bitter blow,
I'll tell you what you need to know;
It's simple as the songs of spring,
as subtle as what rainbows bring.

Let's say your morning starts out bad,
a better hair day you have had.
The doctor lets you sit for hours.
You've fallen from those ivory towers.

Your uncle died, your husband fled,
a meager life so far you've led.
Your mother-in-law stays for weeks,
or someone else your body seeks.

Well, let me put your mind at ease,
and your frustrations I'll appease;
for though this life fits in a journal
the answer is that life's eternal.

And all this here is a testing ground.
For it's your soul that will abound.
And too, another soul stands near
to be your guardian while you're here.

And if you know this you can play,
and you can go, or you can stay.
For know, the soul that dwells in you
has much non-earthly things to do.

It's here to merely play a role
It's God-like, it's a stately soul.
It's in the image of the One
it took the form of man for fun.

And games your guardian plays above;
and he can push or he might shove.
But all in fun and all a test,
and all to see which souls can rest.

And that be those who love, no doubt;
it's those who shall go no more out.

                                                    Rev. 3:12

## A Prophesy (I)

Though quenched by the rain
                     of God;
we will drown by the reign
                     of man.

## View from This Side

Upon this burdened world I view
the scattered feeble numbers,
the few whom God will surely call
to dwell within His chambers.

There's few who seem to know the score;
the reason for their being.
The door to everlasting life
seems not within their seeing.

We're merely pawns and this I'll tell
for angelic spirit creatures
who dwell within our body forms
and let life be their teachers.

## The Card (I)

Let it come to pass
that in the lightness
of this Christmas morn,
God's smile will rise
and touch the hearts
of all man;
that the tenderness
in our being
be all that remain.

## A Prophesy (II)

The battles which our fathers fought
it seems today they should have not.
For in which spiral life evolves,
around the sun and moon revolves,
I see a scant light mixed within
the hollow of the growing sin.
And life without the love of God
shall wither in the fertile sod,
should perish 'neath His lightning rod.

# Friendships

I see the storm clouds slowly forming.
I see dim distant lightning performing.
The gray sky reaching for the blue,
the sound of thunder passing thru.

I live each day as life might lead it.
I do not nurse, or fund, or feed it.
Its course goes in and out of love
I feel its path came from above.

And though be planned, I must beware
and pause thru life and live in prayer;
appreciating each soul's touch
in this short stay we love so much.

Yes, this short stay which God has granted
was not for hate nor strife intended,
but for this time, God has revealed
that life and love was heaven sealed.

I see the gray clouds dissipating,
my heart beats fast anticipating.
Though all the loved ones yet to touch
I'd trade for past ones, loved so much.

# The Tree

I'll bet when God first made the tree
He had an afterthought;
then changed and re-arranged her leaves,
it's likely as it's not.

He probably started with the elm
and loved her towering strength;
then sat and gazed upon her face,
her age to any length.

Then slowly plucked He off a leaf
and floated it to earth;
and from the place on which it lit
a balsam came to birth.

He smiled and plucked another
and planted He a pine;
and moments later at His feet
the newborn count was nine.

Then birch and oak and aspen came;
green covered all the land.
He twitched His beard and wondered
should more color be at hand?

So He snipped the top leaf, sweetened it,
and touched it to the ground;
and red and amber maple's gold
and orange spread all around.

Then satisfied, He took His leave
to sit among the stars,
to smile upon His splendid work
His elbow rest on Mars.

Then suddenly He realized
their offspring lacked the sun.
He stiffened, scratched His neck and knew
that something must be done.

"A time," He said, "a time must come
when each of you must fall
to make room for your children
to take root and grow tall."

So, the beetle, worm, and beaver spread,
requiring a need.
They took the tree's life sparingly
and left the tiny seed.

Then wind and fire God commands
will also play a part
to reassure a changing flow
where each new tree could start.

And finally man fulfills a role,
they cut and strip her bark;
for warmth and shelter from the cold
not to mention Noah's ark!

## Our Struggle

Yea Lord, how precious time is,
this I know;
how quickly life's amiss.
We trace the tracks
of which you left
yet lose you in the mist.

# The Visit (I)

The Lord stopped by the house today . . .
and oh, so, unexpected;
the bed unmade and I'm afraid
the dishes were neglected.

He said that if the coffee's on
a moment He could spare.
I quickly thought, *There's half a pot,
clean cups and silverware.*

I cleared the table and my throat.
I thought it truly odd.
And who'll think me sane
when I explain,
that I had supped with God!

## Letter to Pamela

Dear lady,

The arrow of this letter points to the welcome of this new child's soul. Let fate be its reason for return and let love be its teacher and kindness be its mark. You have conceived thru the will of our Master and you were chosen above all to carry and coddle and rear this child of reason. You have been given a friend of the highest level. He will carry your name, your eyes, and your smile. So let your smile be his morning and your eyes reflect the love he requires. Cast to the night all thoughts of misfortune, for the road in the mirror has no bearing on your goal. Be in truth with this child, for if he sees no shame, he will learn not its meaning. And be at peace with yourself, for the sights of life's meaning aim only at happiness, friendship, and love,

Ron

# A Prophesy (III)

Throughout this mystery of life
God's sacred words lie deep within
and correspond with kindness,
yet shudder "midsthisin."

## The Coming

Lord, what is this really all about?
We're set to self destruct, no doubt.
All weapons that were made for war
have all been used, at least so far,
less now the weapon of today
that's made to wipe us all away.
I watch our leaders meet to chat
and yet deep down I'm knowing that
our days go fast and days are few
before a west wind passing through
has with it particles of fate
and scents of love changed into hate.
And you and I just sit and wait . . .
And you and I just sit and wait . . .

## The Statement

Blessed, in truth, are these
manifestations as to which
all glory seeketh, though all
that shine are hidden by
shadows of beastly beings.
Mellow, in hope, for equality
in understanding and desideratum
of all principles unduly reiterates
the decisions held once so
strong and dear.
Final forward motion is feared
                         by
                               all.

## Our Stay

There's another spirit waiting in the wings,
and when your time comes 'round you will be told;
and if there's not an urgent fervent need,
it hopefully will wait till you are old.

For when that ageless Michael calls your name,
and Jesus finds you written in the book,
the gates will open wide and hide all shame
into the depths of heaven you will look.

So, in the meantime if you know 'tis true,
and Christ is safely tucked within your heart;
then you'll live and give in peace during your stay
and love will be your shadow 'til you part.

## A Christmas Letter

Christmas sneaks to our doors once again and oh, if it doesn't seem to want to come in. And so we respond with lights ablaze and buy for the children the latest craze. We'll hang up those stockings so Santa will see, (and hope this time around he won't forget me). Well, let's make it fun and let's keep it merry with carols and candles and hearts that are cheery. Yet let's pause and remember and keep in our thought; it's the birth of our Savior, let our children be taught. It's that which we honor; He was born of this earth; as the Christ he arrived. It's the Christ child's birth.

## The Separation

Line my tomb with daffodils
but weep no tear for me.
Let the willow shade my face this day
and keep me company.

The only goals I sought in life
were love and laughter's smile;
the only tears I want this day
are raindrops for awhile.

My life shown short in terms of years
but long in happiness.
The tender touch of loved ones' hearts
has left me full of bliss.

So, loved ones when I leave this day
be it not a day of mourn;
for this body was made to decay away
but my soul was heaven born.

So, I'll leave you and thank you
and kiss your face,
for my life with you now ends.
But our souls will unite
in the hand of God
when the bow of heaven bends.

# Mary

Come sit in comfort upon the pews and I shall tell of the latest news. There's a biblical woman I've read about, was a special lady there is no doubt. Word has it she obtained the umbilical cord of Jesus our Savior, the Christ, our Lord. It had lain those years anointed in oil of spikenard to preserve and keep it from spoil.

Was the old Hebrew woman which Joseph besought, and quick as he could to the cave he brought. But oh, too late, for at Mary's breast was the Son of our Father, the utmost best.

So, the Hebrew woman, sly as a fox, placed the cord in an alabaster box. Till many years later it came to suffice, for Mary Magdalene to be more precise. And with this same oil, quite valued by some, she washed the feet of our favored One.

She, with her sister, watched as Jesus raised their dead brother, one Lazarus. She watched Christ pass by bearing the cross. She witnessed His death, our greatest loss. And she was the first to view Him there mistook as a gardener so tall and fair.

So, to tell the truth through my own eyes, she would have taken a Nobel Prize. And if I were Catholic this thought I'd embrace; both Mary the mother and this Mary grace.

## My Psalm

The Lord is my woodland, I shall want no more. He asks that I sit 'neath this oak tree. I quench myself from His cool waters. He relates to my soul. He grants me to cut a clear path to my fields in His namesake. Yea, though I walk thru my land in the blackness of night I will fear not, for thou are a part of me. My bow and my arrow they comfort me. I shall erect a small building just for Him in the presence of my assessor. My heart spilleth over. Surely, goodness and pleasure shall follow me all the days I live here for I am dwelling in the house of the Lord till He takes me, forever.

## In Passing

I watched him slipping slow away, a drawing to your side. And oh, what better place to stay; in Your loving arms abide.

## The Storm

Not by chance she arrived
on the wings of the Snows
and trampled us
like a million white stallions.

To show us her strength
she demolished our power;
our manmade wires
and our ivory towers.
She turned us to darkness
with the whine of her wind song.

She stopped man in his tracks
and then with a whisper
erased his existence;
and with each fading footstep
blindly stumble for shelter
from one remaining
and living reminder
of one of God's treasures
that man cannot conquer.

## Of Loving

So it's in the glow of indigo
your love comes shimmering on.
Just as the past was settled dust
you cast your spell upon.

Beyond all hopes expectancy;
outreaching all that's known.
Beseeching all that's taught to teach,
enchanting that what's grown.

And so, devotion nestles
in its own peculiar way.
It stretches, yawns, and smiles upon
then snuggles in to stay.

And with it rides all caring
with kindness close beside;
till He should call, who saved us all,
to go with Him abide.

# The Card (II)

May Christmas dance about you
singing and its spirit, holy, linger,
long after in your heart.

## Two Towers

The bombs dropped by—they broke the sky, the silent, silken air. And everyone was set aback and all did seem to care. They were not bombs the book of Psalms had written of as fate—just planes of people passing by we realized too late. And in the fear that dawn drew near the passengers were taken. And in the moments that did pass the whole of us were shaken. With only knives they took their lives then took three thousand more. And we stepped back in disbelief and called them acts of war. And in our grief and disbelief we sent our ships a-sailing. Our soldiers in their uniforms knew not the word called "failing." Our jets, they scream and leave their stream of vapor on the wind. We drew the battle lines in sand and aim at those who sinned. And be it known, that which is sown, shall all the guilty reap—'til Jesus in his loving arms shall all his servants sweep.

# **Letting Go**
*(Ode to Carolyn)*

I have trusted all I have to Him;
to He who cleanses me of all sin.
To He who guides eternal light;
who sees all wrong and loves all right.

I know Him well, I've seen His smile
come in to spell me for awhile;
as struggling, I, to beat defeat
had asked His presence to compete.

Then swift as angel wings unfurl
and as the goddess wind will swirl,
to my delight I see Him near
and watch all sadness disappear.

I watch and oh, His vision bright
has with it hints of heaven's light.
And I, to honor such a scene,
embrace His love with none between;
embrace His love with none between.

## November

Yea Lord, I've watched November
swiftly flee. Wow, barely time for turkey.
I got my deer, a ten-point buck;
it's now but steaks and jerky.

## The Visit (II)

The Lord stopped in yet while I slept.
He touched upon my shoulder.
I jumped and recognized His face,
For He did not look older.

I shook the dreams from in my head.
I blinked to clear my vision.
I sat upon the bed beside
our Savior who had risen.

I said, "My Lord, what brings you by
so early in the morn?
I do not look my best to greet
the Christ from virgin born."

He ran His fingers through His beard.
He seemed as deep in thought.
He glowed in loving, living light—
His glory I had caught.

I shivered as He raised His hand
and softly raised His voice.
He said, "It seems you're troubled, son;
I came, I had no choice."

"I have no more important thing
than to comfort one who grieves;
whose loses sleep and loses soul
yet in myself believes."

"So, live in peace, be troubled not
for I'm always within reach.
And if allowed, I'll guide your path
and all your seasons teach."

## Fact or Friction

There is something most don't realize
so let us sit and analyze:
We'll live our lives in fiction
until we learn of friction.
For no matter what you say or do
it's friction that will lead you through.

The feelings when you kiss and such
are friction on that part you touch.
The automobile that you pride
can indicate a suicide;
and yet the truth when but unfold,
a bearing froze, the grease was old.
Or when one runs for president
you know quite well the message sent
is geared to grind a graying hue
for right and wrong cause friction too.

There's times when you will think you've won
when yet in fact you've just begun.
For it doesn't matter what you do,
it's friction that will see you through.

The train that starts the yearly fire;
oh, friction with its deadly choir.
Or strike the wheel against the flint,
it's friction flamed so get the hint.
It doesn't matter who you sue
it's friction that will see you through.

What brings our shuttle to a halt
but friction, brakes unless a fault;
or tear the tiles off her helm
again it's friction overwhelm.
See it doesn't matter where you go
it's friction whether fast or slow.

It's something sent from up above.
It's what makes kids when you make love.
It's friction that will see you through,
it's He who sent it unto you.

## Preparations

November left without a sign
and planted Christmas on my mind.
There's presents, love, and trees to buy;
and now more ham and pumpkin pie.
And what for Uncle Ted to get.
He hasn't liked one present yet.
And back and forth we'll pace these halls
with tinkle and tinsel and Christmas balls.
With carols and laughter that fill the hearts
of the passers-by who play their parts.
And all for the sake of a favored Son,
our Lord and Savior our one to one;
our Lord and Savior our one to one.

# The Vision

I sat beneath a massive elm
and from a distance viewed
upon this vast humanity
all vain and rash and rude.

I saw the Stalin massacre
that did not make the news.
I saw how Hitler influenced
to kill ten million Jews.

I watched as man loved man and died.
I've seen how one can hate.
The hand of God I fear will slide
and man eradicate.

But when? The question's seldom asked
for fear of the unknown.
For in His vision first is last
and few good seeds were sown.

And so I rose and with the wind
I left the elm behind.
I know that all of man has sinned,
and most of man are blind.

## Jesus Was a Cowboy

Jesus was a cowboy once.
I met Him on the plains.
He rode a pinto, brown and white.
He never touched the reins.

That pony did what our Lord thought,
like he knew it in advance.
He galloped, cantered, walked and stood;
at times would even prance.

I rode with Him in Idaho
where we was punchin' cattle.
We rode together right on past
that Custer fellow's battle.

We crossed the fields near Omaha.
I's with Him quite a spell.
He often talked what heaven's like
but rarely spoke of hell.

We stopped quite parched at one saloon
but all He drank was wine—
Me, well I had a beer and bump;
He seemed to think that fine.

Then one day at a setting sun
He said He'd things to do.
He told me I could tag along,
I knew that wasn't true.

My horse would never keep with His,
I think that mustang flies.
I said, "No thanks, I'm heading south,"
and mumbled other lies.

And there we parted company
though I kept Him in my heart.
And as He headed west to east
I felt a teardrop start.

Then as I watched Him ride away
I saw what came to pass,
He, high atop a pinto where
last time He rode an ass!

## The Glow

I pause to look upon your face
in peaceful slumber, dreaming;
and realize in truth that you
are all, in God's light, gleaming.

## The Rapture

So, what is it has happened
to this whole lewd human race?
We're born into such beauty
but of this we'll leave no trace.

Where brother avenge brother
for a sake that has no cause.
And nation against nation
and there never seems a pause.

I know the light is shining
when I view the evening sky.
It's He who'll come to save the world
and I know the reason why.

To preserve His Father's labor;
He will come upon His toil,
and pick the seeds most rightly fit
and let the others spoil.

## The Trade

I asked the Lord to be my strength,
to carry all the weight.
He said, "That isn't why you're here,
move on, you're running late."

And so, bewildered on I trekked
with all my burdens bore.
A window He had seemed to close
but opened up a door.

And in I went, and there you were,
and now my load you share.
So with it carry all my love
and your burdens I will bear.

## Shields

Oh blessed angel guardians
bring your wings in low,
and shelter those this Christmas
who have nowhere to go.

# The Parable

The Lord said, "Son, let's take a walk."
Our pace seemed rather slow.
He said, "I think we need to talk."
His voice was soft and low.

"There are reasons why each soul is here;
in purpose they return.
I hold each one within me dear
and yours gives me concern.

"You see, a goal is laid for you;
your reason on this earth.
Perhaps to save a soul or two
or merely to give birth.

"But you," He said, I swallowed hard,
"have not your purpose found.
You go thru life somewhat on guard
and your feet stay on the ground.

"Get on that path that takes you far,"
He said with eyes aglow.
"And when you see that distant star
you'll know which way to go."

And then He left, so quick He fled
I barely saw Him leave.
But now my soul, whose shell has shed,
will to some purpose cleave.

## Weaver

Well, as the northern dancing lights
bring awe with their display,
you too are awesome in my sight
your smile can make my day.

And each fall softly sheds its leaves
as warmth gives way to cold.
While you and I, the Master weaves,
together to grow old.

# Crucifixion

Most times my own days
I could to the winds toss.
But this was the day
Christ was nailed to the cross.

So in honor I'm telling
oh you of my peer
of just what can happen
when one instills fear.

They whipped Him and scourged Him
and spat in His eye.
And He never did whimper
and He never did cry.

He hoisted the cross
to His shoulders and walked.
and the bystanders hollered
and prodded and mocked.

One placed a crown
of thorns on His head.
But no scar would remain
from where He had bled.

Then they hung up a sign
that said "King of the Jews."
And oh had they known
He was paying their dues.

Then they raised Him on high.
With nails they secured.
And but for the love
of us all He endured.

But no one could harm Him
until the ninth hour,
when God touched His son
and withdrew His power.

Then He gasped a few words
no one understood.
Then He gave up the ghost
as He had said He would.

Yes, He died for our sins;
He carried the load.
Then He headed on back
to His Father's abode.

And I'll tell you my friends
He waits there for us,
so long as we smile,
love, repent, and don't cuss.

## Of Christmas (I)

The birthday of our Lord arrived
so swift as left me weary.
It issued in in life's fast pace
in hustled, scurried fury.

I don't think that He meant it this;
I doubt His view's assuring.
We bring the love in picture pure
all wrapped and so alluring.

But this is not the love He meant.
I think His love's not boughten.
I think His love embraces all
yet some have just forgotten.

And so it seems we celebrate
with wished for and with wanted.
The meaning, true, indeed appears
as only riches flaunted.

## Your Gift

I've analyzed and realized
there's something each must do
to purify and classify
this stay we're passing through.

A story read, a kind word said
for reasons unto God;
a passion plea, a brave decree
before we're in the sod.

For reasons lie under this sky
that we have been here placed.
To live and love what He above
has granted us and graced.

So, each must clasp and try to grasp
that gift to which we're given.
And play it true, till time is through
and we are blessed with heaven.

## The Thank You

Now for your prayers, and thoughts, and gifts,
we send our thanks, for each uplifts
and calms our griefs and sorrows too
in these sad times we're passing through.

## Of Christmas (II)

So, once again the fortunate will decorate the tree; will seek the gifts of one's desire and sing so merrily. And cards will fill each mailbox and each vision of the child will dance in turn each one to sleep in vivid colors wild. And cheer will flow and lights will glow and hearts will fill with love; and somewhere in the bustle some will pause and glance above; and for a moment realize, and solely without doubt, that Christ's own light, whom some can see, is what it's all about.

## Christmas 2000

Again the seasons hasten on in
and we whom have made it seem frazzled.
The turkey is gone in a couple of meals;
the millennium bug has us dazzled.

The property tax takes its toll on our stash.
Seems what we can spend gets some smaller.
But if our credit card line isn't maxed
we'll buy gifts with every last dollar.

The trees are put up and the lights are put on
and the power plants know we are here.
The neighbors will smile and converse for awhile
though they won't for the rest of the year.

For this is the season of giving of gifts
though no one is really sure why;
for if it's a birthday that we celebrate
our gifts should be mailed to the sky.

Addressed only to Christ, in heaven, level three
where the angels their presence enhance;
where the gift of one's spirit unwrapped in His hands
could surely persuade Him to dance.

## Free Will

Now Jesus during His short stay
has touched us one and all
and you can take His word as truth
or in temptations fall.

For I don't think He's too concerned
though He loves us all it's true.
We have that choice, it's given us,
to love and follow through . . .

Or hate and turn aside from God
and live these lifelong lusts;
which Satan in his earthly form
upon our hearts he thrusts.

And Jesus just leans back and waits
for those that He hears call,
to deliver them unto God's throne
as each, from earth, does fall.

## Vision of a Child

If I die tomorrow, tell you what I'm going to do;
I'm going to go fishin' with Jesus
and maybe take my grandpa too.

I'm going to ask Jesus now first thing
to take me down to a fishin' hole,
where the fish are made of silver
and my fishin' pole is made out of gold.

And we ain't going to take us no old boat
and we ain't going to take no oars.
We'll just walk on out on the waters
as if the waters was made out of floors.

And I'll cast with a lure made of diamonds
and I'll cast with a lure made of stones.
And I'll catch me a limit of crappies
and I'll fillet them without any bones.

Then Jesus, with a smile, will tell me,
"Son, we better get off of the lake,
'cuz the loved ones that died before you
are waiting with ice cream and cake."

Yes, if I die tomorrow, that's what I'm going to do,
I'm going to go fishin' with Jesus
and maybe take my uncle too;
and maybe take my grandma too.
I'll take all my past loved ones too.

## My Shelter from the Storm

I'm walking light on air, my feet don't touch the ground
I'm thinking now the reason is 'cuz you're around.
You came into my life and now brighter seem the stars
and everything that's mine is now ours.

Together we can build a bonding love that can't be
 broke.
Together we fulfill the needs of which the Bible spoke.

I sat upon the balcony of life's estate.
I wandered down that long lonely interstate.
And in this pettiness of time I've passed on many
 schemes,
and now you stand at the gate of all my dreams.

You take the flower from your hair, your beauty grows.
The northern lights dance freely as your loving shows.
A chilling wind comes sifting in but you're keeping my
 heart warm,
you'll always be my shelter from the storm.

And together we can build a bonding love that can't be
 broke.
Together we fulfill the needs of which the Bible spoke.